AFRICA

Go Exploring! Continents and Oceans

By Steffi Cavell-Clarke

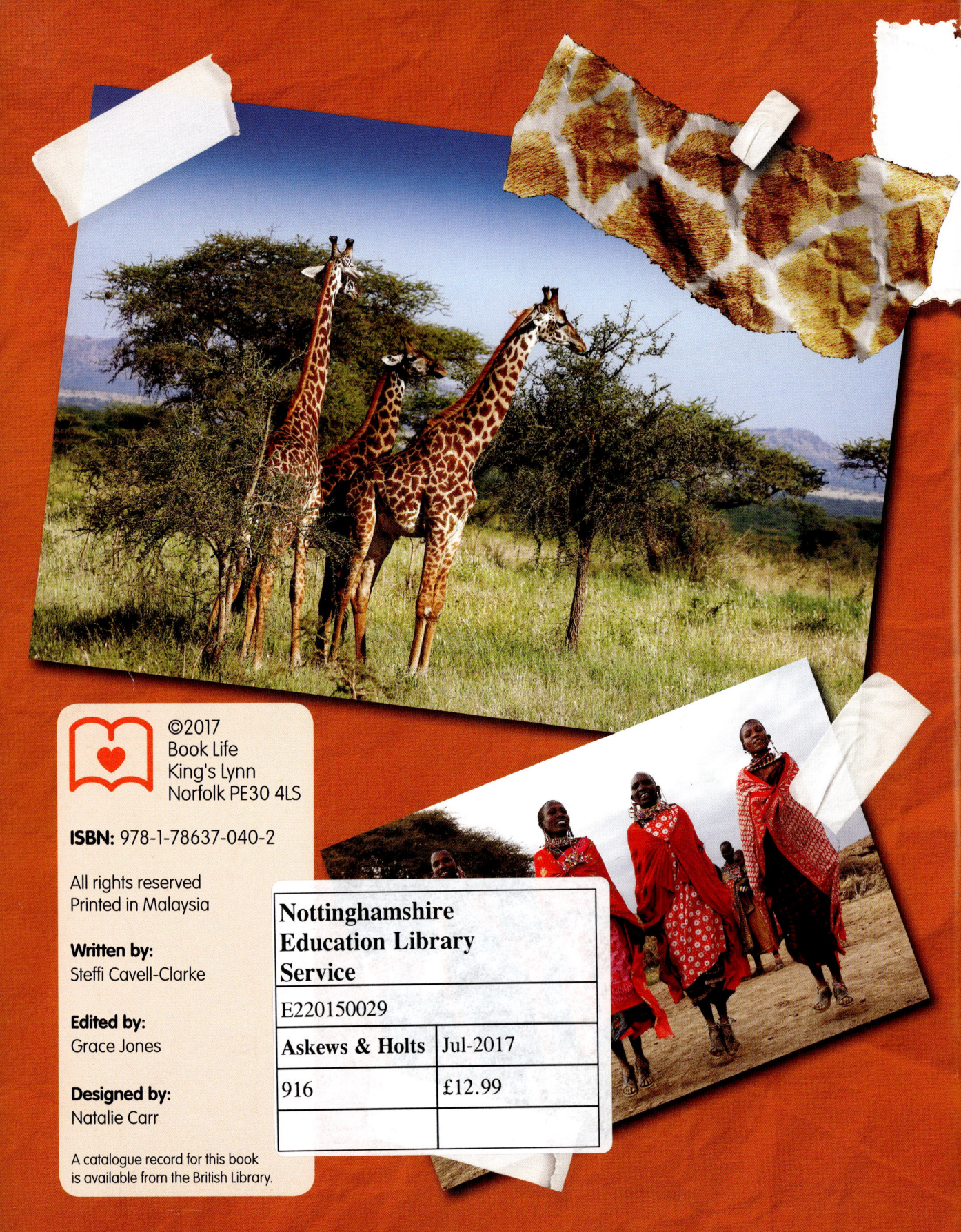

©2017
Book Life
King's Lynn
Norfolk PE30 4LS

ISBN: 978-1-78637-040-2

All rights reserved
Printed in Malaysia

Written by:
Steffi Cavell-Clarke

Edited by:
Grace Jones

Designed by:
Natalie Carr

A catalogue record for this book is available from the British Library.

Nottinghamshire Education Library Service	
E220150029	
Askews & Holts	Jul-2017
916	£12.99

AFRICA

CONTENTS

PAGE 4	What is a Continent?
PAGE 6	Where is Africa?
PAGE 8	Oceans
PAGE 10	Countries
PAGE 12	Weather
PAGE 14	Landscape
PAGE 18	Wildlife
PAGE 20	Settlements
PAGE 22	The Environment
PAGE 23	Glossary
PAGE 24	Index

Words in red can be found in the glossary on page 23.

WHAT IS A CONTINENT?

A continent is a very large area of land that covers part of the Earth's surface. There are seven continents in total. There are also five oceans that surround the seven continents.

- NORTH AMERICA
- ARCTIC OCEAN
- EUROPE
- ASIA
- ATLANTIC OCEAN
- AFRICA
- EQUATOR
- SOUTH AMERICA
- INDIAN OCEAN
- AUSTRALIA
- PACIFIC OCEAN
- SOUTHERN OCEAN
- ANTARCTICA

The seven continents are home to the Earth's **population**. Each continent has many different types of weather, landscape and wildlife. Let's go exploring!

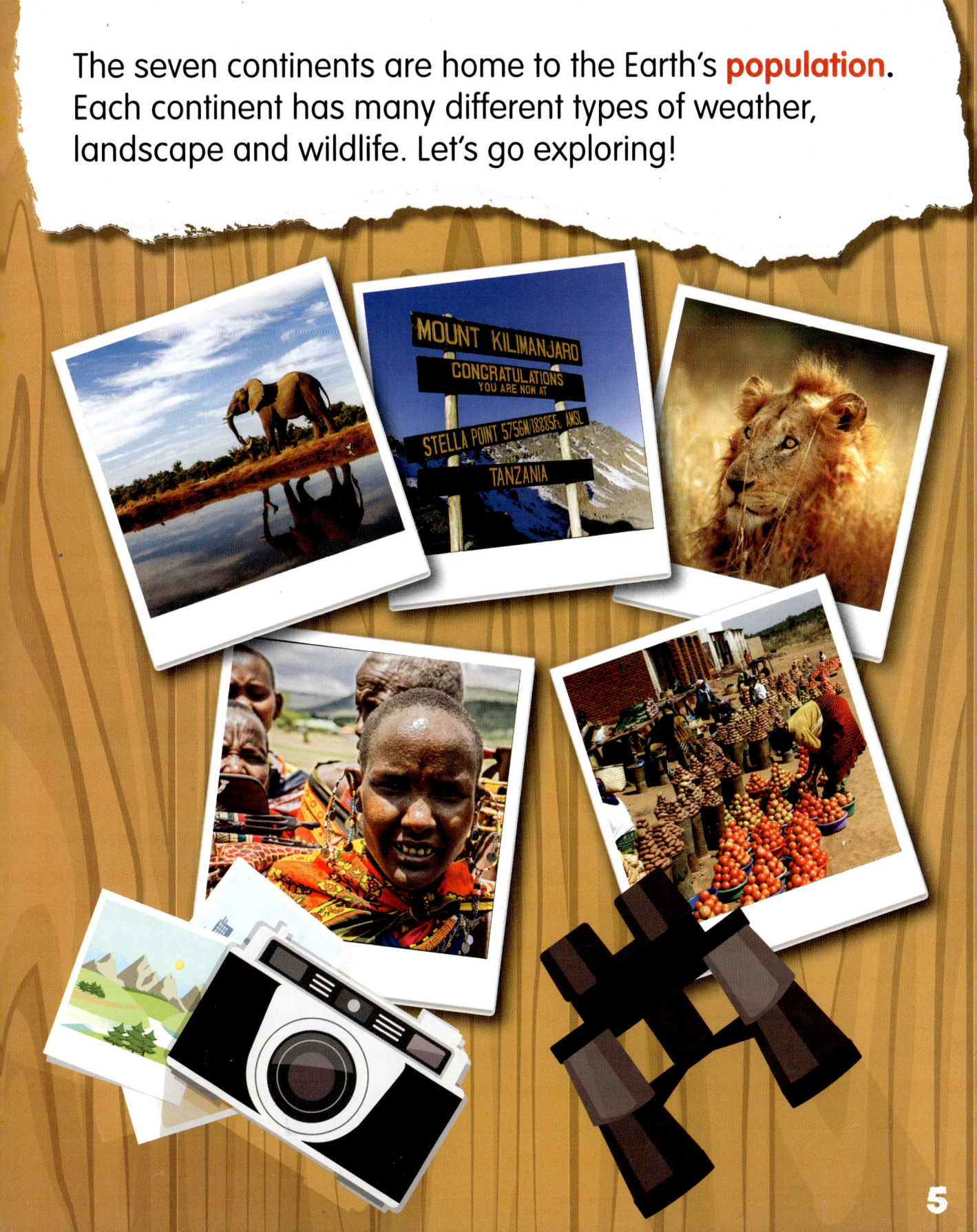

WHERE IS AFRICA?

Africa is the second largest continent in the world. It is **located** south of Europe and Asia, and it is north of Antarctica.

There are two oceans that surround Africa. The Atlantic Ocean is to the west of Africa and the Indian Ocean is to the east.

Atlantic Ocean

Africa

Madagascar

Indian Ocean

6

There are many different countries and landscapes in Africa. The continent also includes lots of small and large islands, which are areas of land completely surrounded by water. The large island of Madagascar lies in the Indian Ocean and is also part of Africa.

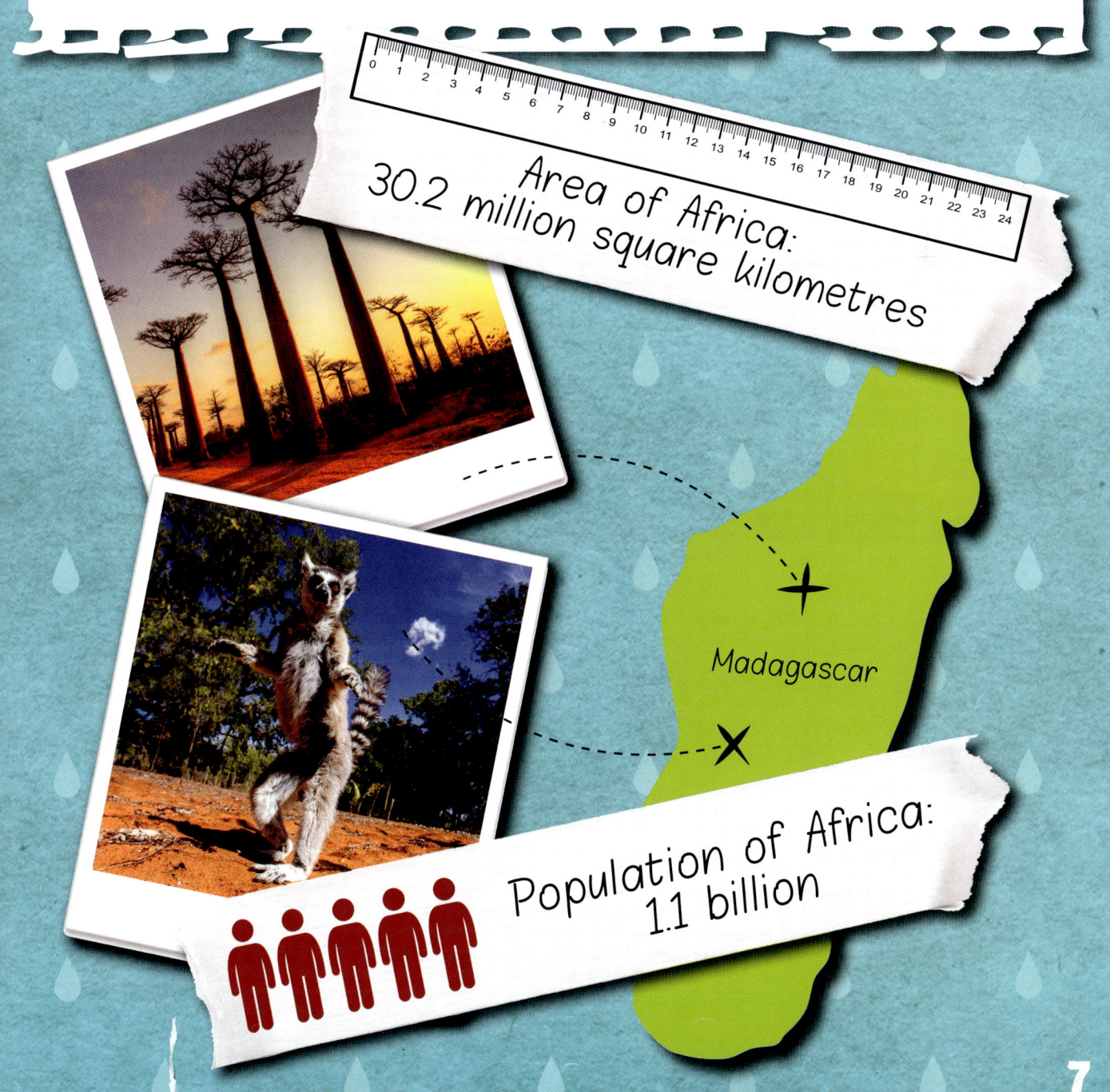

Area of Africa: 30.2 million square kilometres

Population of Africa: 1.1 billion

OCEANS

A sea is an extremely large area of salt water. The biggest seas in the world are called oceans. Just like countries, seas and oceans have different names.

Africa is mostly surrounded by the Atlantic Ocean, Indian Ocean and other seas.

FACT FILE

Atlantic Ocean:
Area: 15% of Earth's surface
Average Depth: 3,339 metres

Indian Ocean:
Area: 13% of Earth's surface
Average Depth: 3,890 metres

Depth is how deep the water is.

Atlantic Ocean

Indian Ocean

COUNTRIES

There are 55 countries in Africa. Most of them are on the mainland of Africa.

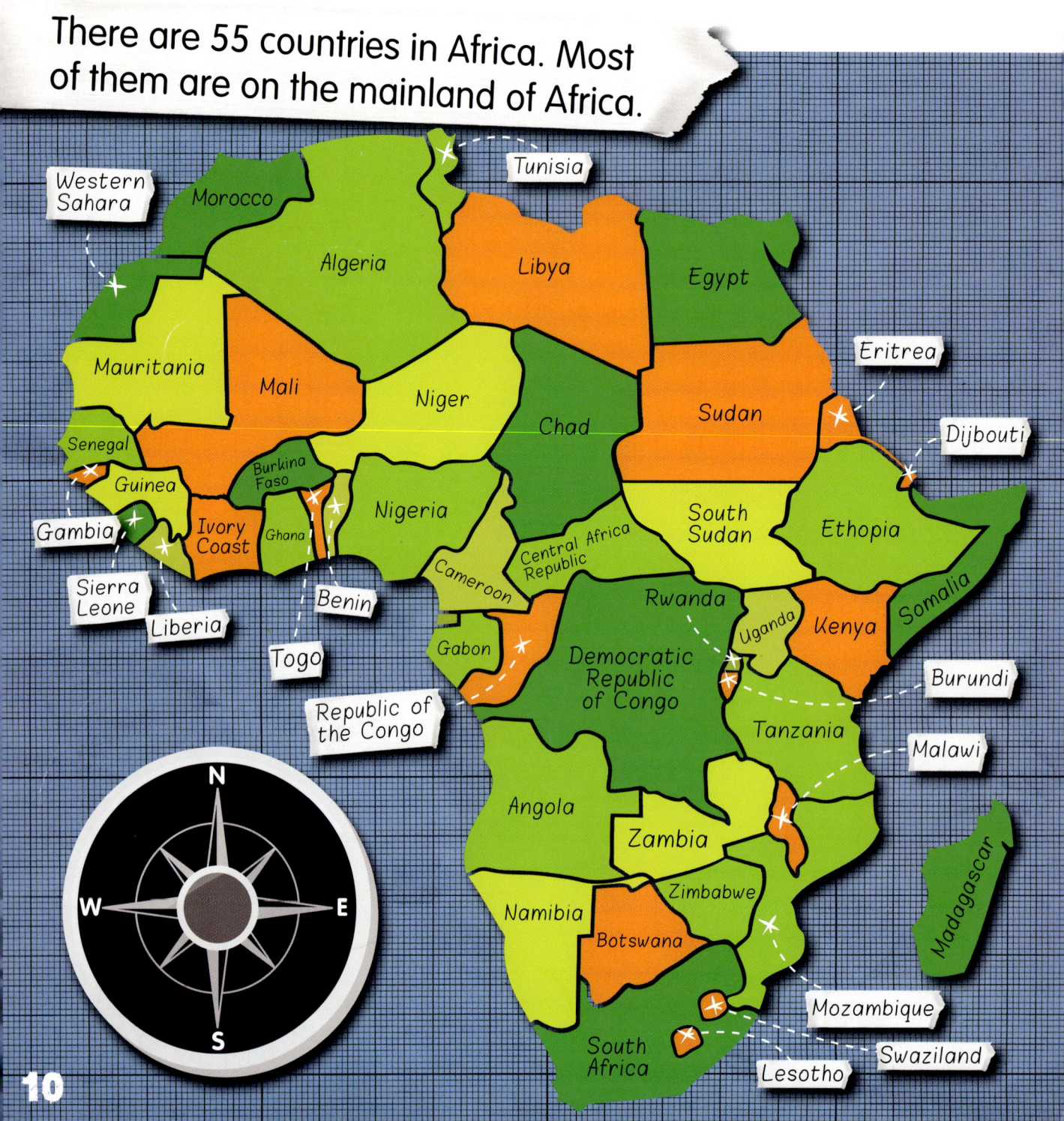

FACT FILE

Largest Country	Algeria	2.38 million square kilometres
Most Populated Country	Nigeria	Over 183 million
Famous Landmark	Ancient Pyramids, Egypt	Over 4,500 years old
Highest Peak	Kilimanjaro, Tanzania	5,895 metres high
Biggest Animal	African Elephant	3 metres tall

11

WEATHER

The **climate** in Africa changes across the continent. The **equator** runs almost directly through the middle of Africa, which is the warmest part of the world. The type of weather on and near to the equator is very warm and wet.

Equator

Africa

Parts of Africa have dry seasons and rainy seasons. In the dry season, it almost never rains and the ground is very dry, but in the rainy season, it rains almost every day. This is also called monsoon season.

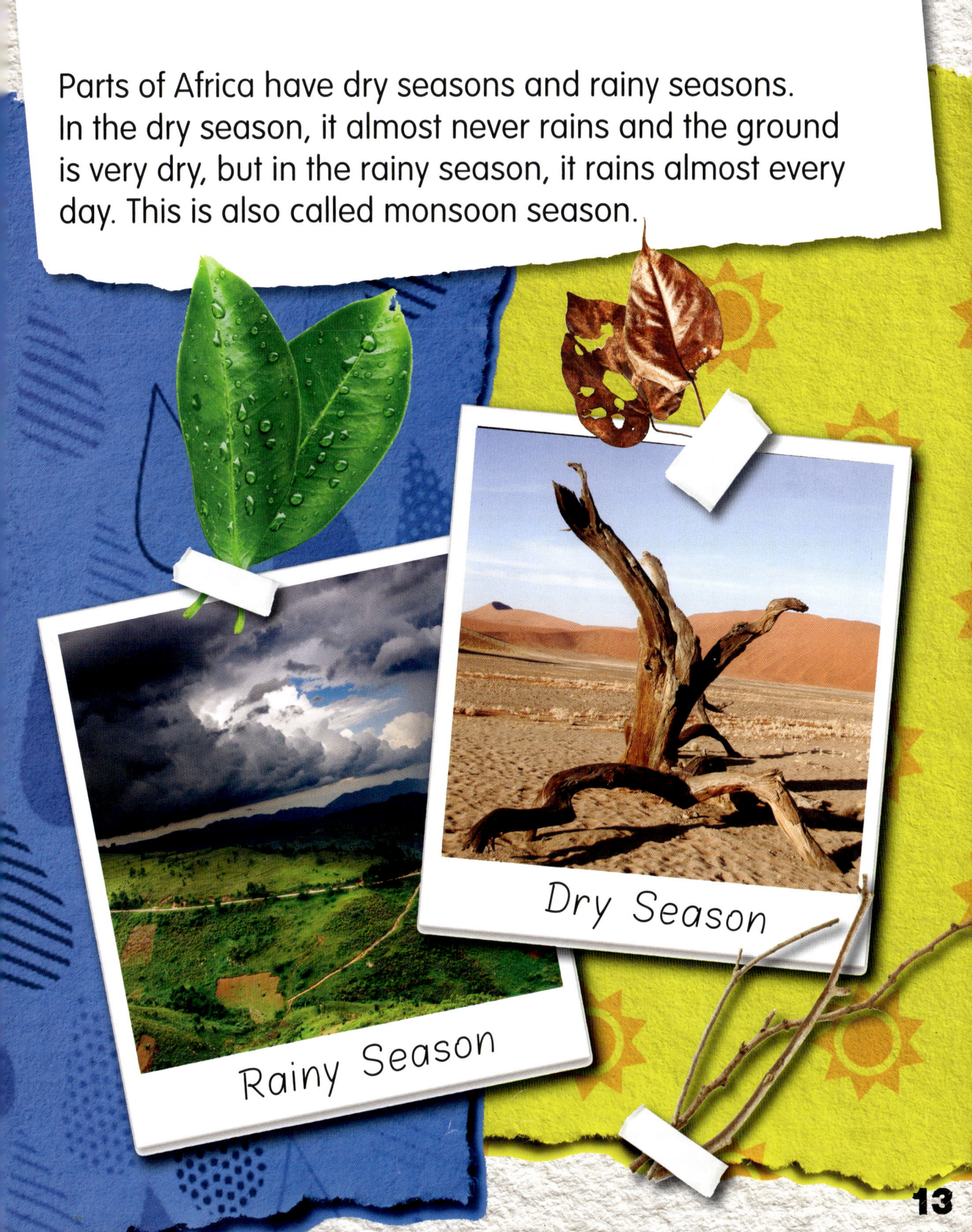

Rainy Season

Dry Season

LANDSCAPE

There are many different types of landscape across Africa. There are large grassy **plains** in central Africa, with hot deserts in the north and **tropical** rainforests in the south. Each landscape has its own climate and wildlife.

African Desert

The tropical rainforest in the Congo has lots of *vegetation* and is home to the mountain gorilla.

There are three deserts on the African continent. They are called the Sahara, Namib and Kalahari.

The Sahara Desert is the largest hot desert in the world. It is 9.4 million square kilometres which covers nearly the whole of north Africa.

Underneath the surface of the Atlantic and Indian Oceans, there are sea beds which are covered in sand, mud and rock. The sea bed has an uneven surface just like land.

Sea Beds

The Atlantic Ocean and Indian Ocean have deep **valleys** in the ground called trenches. The Indian Ocean also has deep caves beneath its surface, which are home to many types of sea life.

WILDLIFE

Africa is home to many beautiful wild animals, such as elephants, giraffes, lions and colourful parrots.

African elephants grow up to 3 metres tall and can weigh up to 6 tonnes!

Lions live in large groups called prides

Parrot Feathers

Elephant in Africa

The blue whale can grow up to 30 metres long!

The blue whale is the largest **mammal** on earth. It lives in both the Atlantic and Indian Oceans.

SETTLEMENTS

There are many big cities on the African continent. The largest city is Cairo in Egypt. In the cities, many people live in tall, modern buildings.

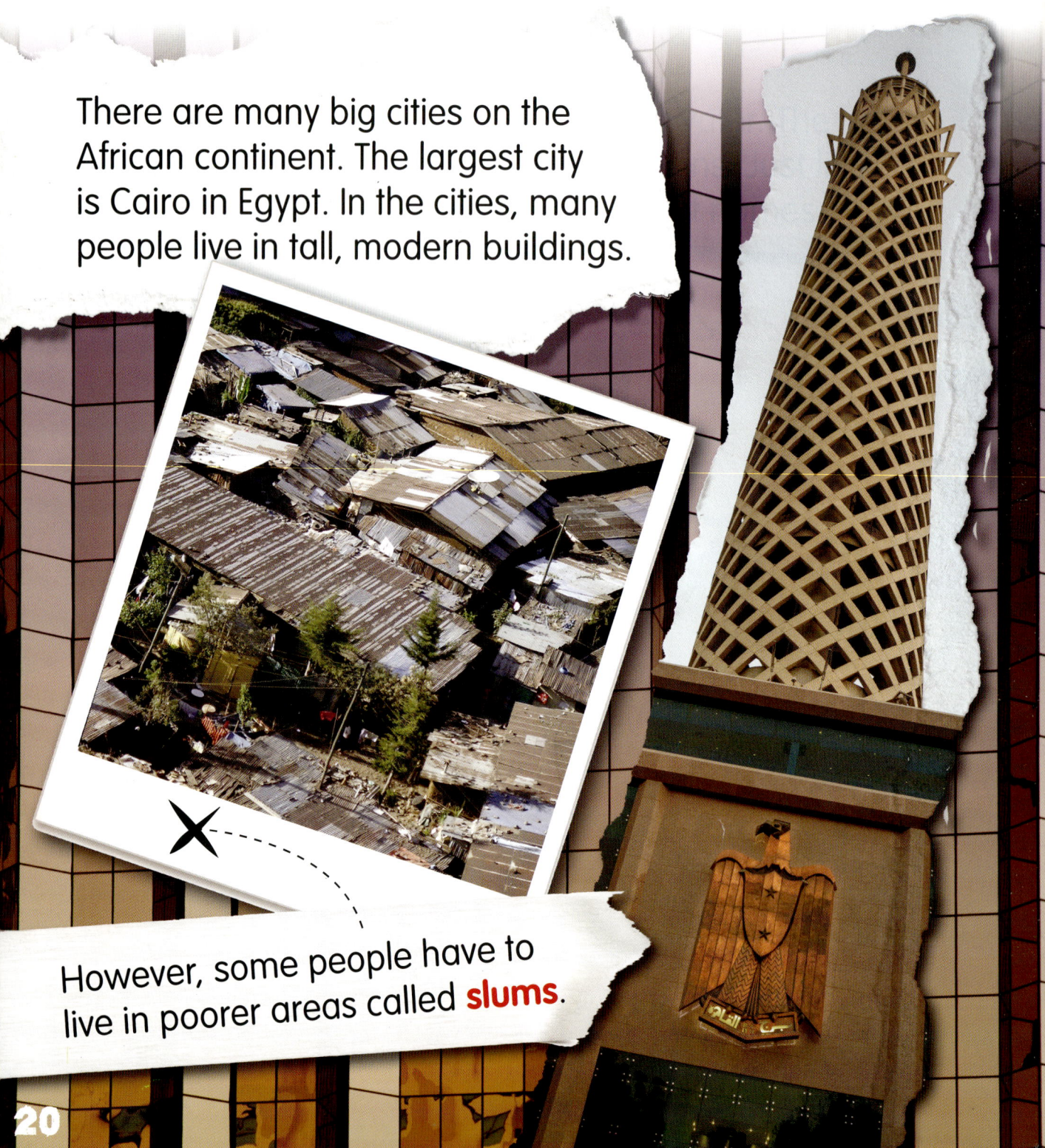

However, some people have to live in poorer areas called **slums**.

Many people in Africa live in the countryside. There are many farming villages where people often grow crops such as sugar cane and herd animals. They can either eat their crops or sell them at the local market.

Sugar Cane Plant

Cattle in Africa

21

THE ENVIRONMENT

Many people in Africa do not have enough clean, safe water to drink. This can cause **poverty** and illness. Other countries across the world have given **aid** to Africa to help people access clean water, but there are still many African people who suffer without it.

Nearly one billion people across the world do not have access to safe water.

GLOSSARY

aid support given to another country, such as food or money
climate the average weather of an area
equator imaginary line running around the middle of the earth
located where something can be found
mammal an animal that has warm blood, a backbone and usually has fur
plains large areas of flat land with a few trees
population number of people living in a place
poverty living with little or no money
slums overcrowded areas with poor living conditions
tropical warm and wet areas near the equator
valleys long, narrow and deep grooves in the land
vegetation types of plant found in an area

INDEX

African elephants 11, 18
animals 11, 14, 18–19, 21
Atlantic Ocean 4, 6, 8–9, 16–17, 19
cities 20
climates 12, 14
continents 4–7, 12, 15, 20
deserts 14–15
earth 4-5, 9, 19
Egypt 10–11, 20
equator 4, 12

farming 21
Indian Ocean 4, 6–9, 16–17, 19
landscapes 5, 7, 14–15
Madagascar 6–7, 10
oceans 4, 6, 8–9, 16–17
populations 5, 7
seasons 13
slums 20
weather 5, 12–13
wildlife 5, 14, 18–19

PHOTOCREDITS

Abbreviations: l–left, r–right, b–bottom, t–top, c–centre, m–middle.

Front Cover Background – Flas100. Front Cover Vectors – elenabsl. Front Cover m – Pichugin Dmitry. 2t – Andrzej Kubik. 2tr – bonga1965. 2br – Oleg Znamenskiy. 3tr – Mike Dexter. 3br – Johan Swanepoel. 4tl – elenabsl. 5bl– elenabsl. 5bm – Nick Fox. 5bm – Dennis Albert Richardson. 5tl - Mike Dexter. 5tm – David Evison. 5tr – Johan Swanepoel. 6br – Shinelu. 6 background – Irtsya. 7 background – Irtsya. 7bl – GUDKOV ANDREY. 7tl – Dennis van de Water. 8 background – gudinny. 9 background – taviphoto. 9m – 89studio. 10bl – elenabsl. 10 background – Taigi. 11 background – schab. 11 – Picsfive. 12 background – Igor Kovalchuk. 12m – AridOcean. 12br – MartinMaritz. 13 background l – Mikhaylova Liubov 13b – Pichugin Dmitry. 13m – Tim UR. 13background r – LvNL. 13m – Jokdev. 13m – Mila Supinskaya. 13 background – schab. 14 background – nelik. 14ml – GUDKOV ANDREY. 14mr –marzia franceschini. 15 background – pinyoj. 15tl – Pichugin Dmitry. 15lm – Eniko Balogh. 15lb – Artush. 16 background – schab. 16tl – frantisekhojdysz. 16tr – Jolanta Wojcicka. 16bm – Jolanta Wojcicka. 16br – Carlos Rondon. 16lm – Carlos Rondon. 17t – James Steidl. 17b – Andrzej Kubik. 17 background – Markovka. 18bl – MustafaNC. 18br – Mike Dexter. 18mr – J Reineke. 18 background – val lawless. 19t – jamesteohart. 19 background – Flas100. 20 background – oleandra. 20r – lexan. 20ml – Jan Martin Will. 21 background – fantom_rd. 21l – Hywit Dimyadi. 21tr – Gunter Nezhoda. 21br – Aleksandar Todorovic. 22 background – Curly Pat. 22ml – Riccardo Mayer. 22mr – Dietmar Temps.
Images are courtesy of Shutterstock.com. With thanks to Getty Images, Thinkstock Photo and iStockphoto.